RUN WITH THE WOLVES

Take a walk on the wild side

LUCINDA WILDE

ILLUSTRATED BY
ANITA MANGAN

spruce

In a world full of mystical unicorns and cuddly sloths, it can be hard to be a warrior. Meditations on tranquillity and world peace might work for flamingos, but not everybody looks good in pink. Some of us need to walk on the wild side.

Everybody knows the story about the Big Bad Wolf, who lured Little Red Riding Hood from the path of good intentions before eating her grandmother, and the one about the wolf who terrorized the Three Little Pigs in the hope of a bacon breakfast. Wolves have had a bad press throughout history, but why? In each of these stories, all the wolf has done is what a wolf is born to do – feed itself and survive. Wolves are apex predators; they are sexy, super intelligent and highly successful.

DO NOT FEAR THE WOLF.
BE THE WOLF.

Blessed are the meek, for they shall inherit
nothing at all – so the next time the moon is
full, open the window and let it in! It is time
to embrace your inner wolf.

THE LUPINE WAY

Lolling about on a canopied bed thinking whimsical thoughts is all very zen, but the world was conquered by Genghis Khan and Alexander the Great, not Flopsy Bunny and the Flower Children. For every dreamer, there needs to be a do-er, for every gatherer, a hunter. So, if keeping calm is driving you crazy and mindfulness is blowing your mind, remember your yin and yang. We are creatures of winter as well as summer, of darkness as well as light. The warrior lives within us all.

**FOLLOW THE GUIDING PRINCIPLES OF THE
WOLF TO EXCEL THROUGHOUT YOUR LIFE:**

LIVE FULLY. Every day. There is nothing else.
Only in taking risks can we be truly alive.

EMBRACE YOUR INNER FIRE. Stoke it!
Let it roar!

ALWAYS PLAY TO WIN. In a fight to the
death, the second prize is death.

AMBITION IS NOT A DIRTY WORD. There are
things in life it is OK to be passionate about.

STAY FOCUSED. Distraction is the enemy
of success.

Ditch the leotard: wolves do not
do yoga.

Achievers DO, they do not discuss. You won't catch a wolf in a board meeting.

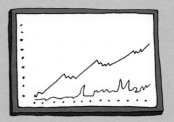

Diversify to survive.
If moose is off the menu,
eat deer. Or pizza.

Wolves do not fear the darkness. Magical things happen by moonlight.

Wolves hunger but do not covet. They do not dream of an upgraded bison.

Wolves do not queue;
they seize opportunity.

Do what you were born
to do. A wolf makes
a poor shepherd.

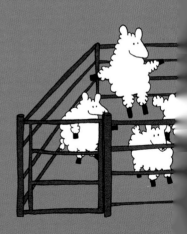

The strength of the wolf is
in its pack and the strength
of the pack is in the wolf.

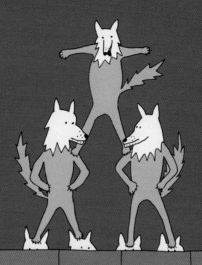

Wolves do not diet.
Empty bellies have
no time for food fads.

A wolf throws its strength against the enemy's weakest point; only a fool headbutts a wall.

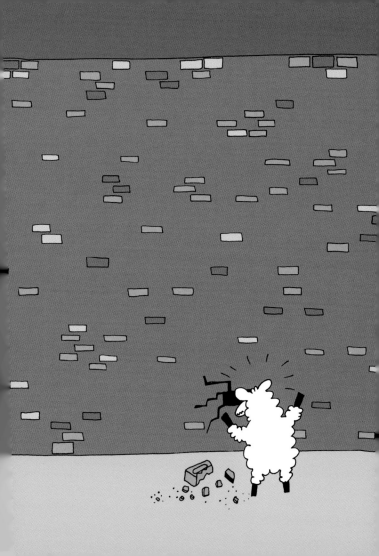

Timing is all. Jump the gun,
lose the prey.

Wolves love fiercely.
The wild is no place
for the faint-hearted.

Even a wolf's best-laid
plans will sometimes
need adjusting.

DEPARTURES

WA 1674	CAIRO	CANCELLED
WA 7003	HAWAII	CANCELLED
WA 6052	SYDNEY	CANCELLED
WA 1674	MUMBAI	CANCELLED
WA 4531	BANGKOK	CANCELLED
WA 3271	WOLVERHAMPTON	CANCELLED
WA 5693	CAPE TOWN	CANCELLED
WA 341	NEW YORK	CANCELLED

A wolf never doubts its importance to the pack.

A wolf does not fear
the opinion of sheep.

A wolf in sheep's clothing
will never look well-dressed.

Wolves are strong enough
to stand alone but wise
enough to stand together.

A cute wolf cub is just
a wolf-in-waiting.

Wolves watch and
learn from their elders.
The wisdom of the pack
is shared wisdom.

In Wolf language, there is no word for 'complain'.

A cautious wolf
lives to be an old wolf.

A wise wolf knows that
sometimes patience and
cunning get the best results.

A wolf does not bite off
more than it can chew.
A full-grown elk is
a sharing platter.

A wounded wolf has
the sharpest fangs.

Wolves do not get bored.
Boredom is a luxury
no wolf can afford.

Wolves are masters
of mindfulness; they do
not regret yesterday or
worry about tomorrow.

Wolves always keep focus.
The wolf that chases two
sheep sleeps hungry.

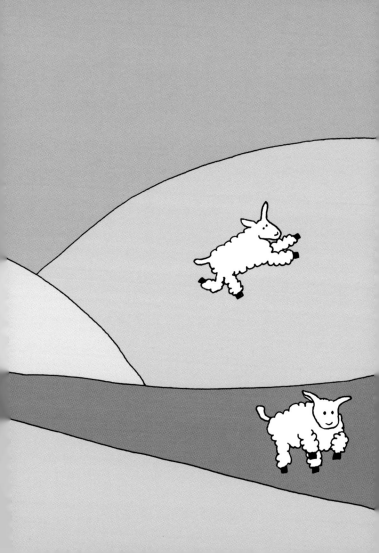

A dog may have a warm place by the fireside, but a wolf wears no chain.

A wolf's only addiction
is the hunt.

You can't teach a wolf
to walk at heel.

A wolf fears no rivals,
it simply removes them.

Wolves do not waste energy
chasing the inedible.

To a wolf, a blizzard is an invitation. In a snowstorm, it is easy to hide.

A wolf finds all the courage
it needs within itself.

If a wolf is outrun by
its dinner, it makes
other arrangements.

Act like a sheep and you will
be eaten by a wolf.

Wolves live in harmony
with the environment.

SUGAR FREE
GLUTEN FREE
DAIRY FREE
ADDITIVE FREE
HIGH PROTEIN
LOW FAT
ORGANIC
FREE RANGE

Now, embrace your inner warrior and run with the wolves!